The Collected Poems and Prose of Jupiter Hammon

The Collected Poems and Prose of Jupiter Hammon

Jupiter Hammon

MINT EDITIONS

The Collected Poems and Prose of Jupiter Hammon were first published between 1760–1787.

This edition published by Mint Editions 2021.

ISBN 9781513282442 | E-ISBN 9781513287461

Published by Mint Editions®

MINT
EDITIONS
minteditionbooks.com

Publishing Director: Jennifer Newens
Design & Production: Rachel Lopez Metzger
Project Manager: Micaela Clark
Typesetting: Westchester Publishing Services

Contents

THE POETRY

An Evening Though: Salvation by Christ, with Penetential Cries

Salvation comes by Jesus Christ alone,
    The only Son of God;
Redemption now to every one,
    That love his holy Word.
Dear Jesus we would fly to Thee,
    And leave off every Sin,
Thy Tender Mercy well agree;
    Salvation from our King.
Salvation comes now from the Lord,
    Our victorious King;
His holy Name be well ador'd,
    Salvation surely bring.
Dear Jesus give they Spirit now,
    Thy Grace to every Nation,
That han't the Lord to whom we bow,
    The Author of Salvation.
Dear Jesus unto Thee we cry,
    Give us the Preparation;
Turn not away thy tender Eye;
    We seek thy true Salvation.
Salvation comes from God we know,
    The true and only One;
It's well agreed and certain true,
    He gave his only Son.
Lord hear our penetential Cry:
    Salvation from above;
It is the Lord that doth supply,
    With his Redeeming Love.
Dear Jesus by thy precious Blood,
    The World Redemption have:
Salvation now comes from the Lord,
    He being thy captive slave.
Dear Jesus let the Nations cry,
    And all the People say,

Salvation comes from Christ on high,
 Haste on Tribunal Day.
We cry as Sinners to the Lord,
 Salvation to obtain;
It is firmly fixt his holy Word,
 Ye shall not cry in vain.
Dear Jesus unto Thee we cry,
 And make our Lamentation:
O let our Prayers ascend on high;
 We felt thy Salvation.
Lord turn our dark benighted Souls;
 Give us a true Motion,
And let the Hearts of all the World,
 Make Christ their Salvation.
Ten Thousand Angels cry to Thee,
 Yea lourder than the Ocean.
Thou art the Lord, we plainly see;
 Thou art the true Salvation.
Now is the Day, excepted Time;
 The Day of Salvation;
Increase your Faith, do no repine:
 Awake ye every Nation.
Lord unto whom now shall we go,
 Or seek a safe Abode;
Thou hast the Word Salvation too
 The only Son of God.
Ho! every one that hunger hath,
 Or pineth after me,
Salvation be thy leading Staff,
 To set the Sinner free.
Dear Jesus unto Thee we fly;
 Depart, depart from Sin,
Salvation doth at length supply,
 The Glory of our King.
Come ye Blessed of the Lord,
 Salvation greatly given;
O turn your Hearts, accept the Word,
 Your Souls are fit for Heaven.

Dear Jesus we now turn to Thee,
    Salvation to obtain;
Our Hearts and Souls do meet again,
    To magnify thy Name.
Come holy Spirit, Heavenly Dove,
    The Object of our Care;
Salvation doth increase our Love;
    Our Hearts hath felt thy fear.
Now Glory be to God on High,
    Salvation high and low;
And thus the Soul on Christ rely,
    To Heaven surely go.
Come Blessed Jesus, Heavenly Dove,
    Accept Repentance here;
Salvation give, with tender Love;
    Let us with Angels share.

An Address to Miss Phillis Wheatly

I

O come you pious youth! adore
    The wisdom of thy God,
In bringing thee from distant shore,
    To learn His holy word.

Eccles. xii.

II

Thou mightst been left behind
    Amidst a dark abode;
God's tender mercy still combin'd,
    Thou hast the holy word.

Psal. cxxxv, 2, 3.

III

Fair wisdom's ways are paths of peace,
    And they that walk therein,
Shall reap the joys that never cease,
    And Christ shall be their king.

Psal. i, 1,2; Prov. iii, 7.

IV

God's tender mercy brought thee here;
    Tost o'er the raging main;
In Christian faith thou hast a share,
    Worth all the gold of Spain.

Psal. cii, 1, 3, 4.

V

While thousands tossed by the sea,
    And others settled down,
God's tender mercy set thee free,
    From dangers that come down.

Death.

VI

That thou a pattern still might be,
    To youth of Boston town,
The blessed Jesus set thee free,
    From every sinful wound.

2 Cor. v, 10.

VII

The blessed Jesus, who came down,
    Unvail'd his sacred face,
To cleanse the soul of every wound,
    And give repenting grace.

Rom. v, 21.

VIII

That we poor sinners may obtain,
    The pardon of our sin;
Dear blessed Jesus now constrain,
    And bring us flocking in.

Psal. xxiv, 6, 7, 8.

IX

Come you, Phillis, now aspire,
  And seek the living God,
So step by step thou mayst go higher,
  Till perfect in the word.

Matth. vii, 7, 8.

X

While thousands mov'd to distant shore,
  And others left behind,
The blessed Jesus still adore,
  Implant this in thy mind.

Psal. lxxxix, 1.

XI

Thou hast left the heathen shore;
  Thro' mercy of the Lord,
Among the heathen live no more,
  Come magnify thy God.

Psal. xxxiv, 1, 2, 3.

XII

I pray the living God may be,
  The shepherd of thy soul;
His tender mercies still are free,
  His mysteries to unfold.

Psal. lxxx, 1, 2, 3.

XIII

Thou, Phillis, when thou hunger hast,
    Or pantest for thy God;
Jesus Christ is thy relief,
    Thou hast the holy word.

Psal. xiii, 1, 2, 3.

XIV

The bounteous mercies of the Lord,
    Are hid beyond the sky,
And holy souls that love his word,
    Shall taste them when they die.

Psal. xvi, 10, 11.

XV

These bounteous mercies are from God,
    The merits of His Son;
The humble soul that loves His word,
    He chooses for His own.

Psal. xxxiv, 15.

XVI

Come, dear Phillis, be advis'd,
    To drink Samaria's flood;
There nothing that shall suffice
    But Christ's redeeming blood.

John iv, 13, 14.

XVII

While thousands muse with earthly toys;
    And range about the street,
Dear Phillis, seek for heaven's joys,
    Where we do hope to meet.

Matth. vi, 33.

XVIII

When God shall send his summons down,
    And number saints together,
Blest angels chant, (triumphant sound),
    Come live with me forever.

Psal. cxvi, 15.

XIX

The humble soul shall fly to God,
    And leave the things of time,
Start forth as 'twere at the first word,
    To taste things more divine.

Matth. v, 3, 8.

XX

Behold! the soul shall waft away,
    Whene'er we come to die,
And leave its cottage made of clay,
    In twinkling of an eye.

Cor. xv, 51, 52, 53.

XXI

Now glory be to the Most High,
    United praises given,
By all on earth, incessantly,
    And all the host of heav'n.

Psal. cl, 6.

A Dialogue Entitled, "The Kind Master and the Dutiful Servant"

MASTER: Come my servant, follow me,
   According to thy place;
   And surely God will be with thee,
   And send the heav'nly grace.
SERVANT: Dear Master, I will follow thee,
   According to thy word,
   And pray that God may be with me,
   And save thee in the Lord.
MASTER: My Servant, lovely is the Lord,
   And blest those servants be,
   That truly love his holy word,
   And thus will follow me.
SERVANT: Dear Master, that's my whole delight,
   Thy pleasure for to do;
   As far as grace and truth's in sight,
   Thus far I'll surely go.
MASTER: My Servant, grace proceeds from God,
   And truth should be with thee;
   Whence e'er you find it in his word,
   Thus far come follow me.
SERVANT: Dear Master, now without controul,
   I quickly follow thee;
   And pray that God would bless thy soul,
   His heav'nly place to see.
MASTER: My Servant, Heaven is high above,
   Yea, higher than the sky:
   I pray that God would grant his love,
   Come follow me thereby.
SERVANT: Dear Master, now I'll follow thee,
   And trust upon the Lord;
   The only safety that I see,
   Is Jesus's holy word.
MASTER: My Servant, follow Jesus now,
   Our great victorious King;

Who governs all both high and low,
And searches things within.
SERVANT: Dear Master I will follow thee,
When praying to our King;
It is the Lamb I plainly see,
Invites the sinner in.
MASTER: My Servant, we are sinners all,
But follow after grace;
I pray that God would bless thy soul,
And fill thy heart with grace.
SERVANT: Dear Master I shall follow then,
The voice of my great King;
As standing on some distant land,
Inviting sinners in.
MASTER: My Servant we must all appear,
And follow then our King;
For sure he'll stand where sinners are,
To take true converts in.
SERVANT: Dear Master, now if Jesus calls,
And sends his summons in;
We'll follow saints and angels all,
And come unto our King.
MASTER: My Servant now come pray to God
Consider well his call;
Strive to obey his holy word,
That Christ may love us all

A Line on the present War.
SERVANT: Dear Master, now it is a time,
A time of great distress;
We'll follow after things divine,
And pray for happiness.
MASTER: Then will the happy day appear,
That virtue shall increase;
Lay up the sword and drop the spear,
And nations seek for peace.
SERVANT: Then shall we see the happy end,
Tho' still in some distress;

That distant foes shall act like friends,
And leave their wickedness.

MASTER: We pray that God would give us grace,
And make us humble too;
Let ev'ry nation seek for peace,
And virtue make a show.

SERVANT: Then we shall see the happy day,
That virtue is in power;
Each holy act shall have its sway,
Extend from shore to shore.

MASTER: This is the work of God's own hand,
We see by precepts given;
To relieve distress and save the land,
Must be the pow'r of heav'n.

SERVANT: Now glory be unto our God,
Let ev'ry nation sing;
Strive to obey his holy word,
That Christ may take them in.

MASTER: Where endless joys shall never cease,
Blest Angels constant sing;
The glory of their God increase,
Hallelujahs to their King.

SERVANT: Thus the Dialogue shall end,
Strive to obey the word;
When ev'ry nation act like friends,
Shall be the sons of God.

Believe me now my Christian friends,
Believe your friend call'd HAMMON:
You cannot to your God attend,
And serve the God of Mammon.

If God is pleased by his own hand
To relieve distresses here;
And grant a peace throughout the the land,
'Twill be a happy year.

'Tis God alone can give us peace;
It's not the pow'r of man:

When virtuous pow'r shall increase,
'Twill beautify the land.

Then shall we rejoice and sing
By pow'r of virtues word,
Come sweet Jesus, heav'nly King,
Thou art the Son of God.

When virtue comes in bright array,
Discovers ev'ry sin;
We see the dangers of the day,
And fly unto our King.

Now glory be unto our God,
All praise be justly given;
Let ev'ry soul obey his word,
And seek the joys of Heav'n.

A Poem for Children with Thoughts on Death

I

O Ye young and thoughtless youth,
    Come seek the living God,
The scriptures are a sacred truth,
    Ye must believe the word.

Eccl. xii. 1.

II

'Tis God alone can make you wise,
    His wisdom's from above,
He fills the soul with sweet supplies
    By his redeeming love.

Prov. iv. 7.

III

Remember youth the time is short,
    Improve the present day
And pray that God may guide your thoughts,
    And teach your lips to pray.

Psalm xxx. 9.

IV

To pray unto the most high God,
    And beg restraining grace,
Then by the power of his word
    You'l see the Saviour's face.

Little children they may die,
    Turn to their native dust,
Their souls shall leap beyond the skies,
    And live among the just.

VI

Like little worms they turn and crawl,
    And gasp for every breath.
The blessed Jesus sends his call,
    And takes them to his rest.

VII

Thus the youth are born to die,
    The time is hastening on,
The Blessed Jesus rends the sky,
    And makes his power known.

Psalm ciii. 15.

VIII

Then ye shall hear the angels sing
    The trumpet give a sound,
Glory, glory to our King,
    The Saviour's coming down.

Matth. xxvi. 64.

IX

Start ye saints from dusty beds,
    And hear a Saviour call,
'Twas a Jesus Chirst that died and bled,
    And thus preserv'd thy soul.

X

This the portion of the just,
  Who lov'd to serve the Lord,
Their bodies starting from the dust,
  Shall rest upon their God.

XI

They shall join that holy word,
  That angels constant sing,
Glory, glory to the Lord,
  Hallelujahs to our King.

XII

Thus the Saviour will appear,
  With guards of heavenly host,
Those blessed Saints, shall then declare,
  'Tis Father, Son and Holy Ghost.

Rev. i. 7, 8.

XIII

Then shall ye hear the trumpet sound,
  The graves give up their dead,
Those blessed saints shall quick awake,
  And leave their dusty beds.

Matth. xxvii. 51, 52.

XIV

Then shall you hear the trumpet sound,
  And rend the native sky,
Those bodies starting from the ground,
  In the twinkling of an eye.

I Cor. xv. 51, 52, 53, 54.

XV

There to sing the praise of God,
    And join the angelic train,
And by the power of his word,
    Unite together again.

XVI

Where angels stand for to admit
    Their souls at the first word,
Cast sceptres down at Jesus feet
    Crying holy holy Lord.

XVII

Now glory be unto our God
    All praise be justly given,
Ye humble souls that love the Lord
    Come seek the joys of Heaven.

Hartford, January 1, 1782.

THE PROSE

An Address to the Negroes in the State of New York

To the Members of the African Society
in the city of New York Gentlemen,
I take the liberty to dedicate an address to my poor brethren to
you. If you think it is likely to do good among them, I do not
doubt but you will take it under your care. You have discovered
so much kindness and good will to those you thought were
oppressed, and had no helper, that I am sure you will not
despise what I have wrote, if you judge it will be of any service
to them. I have nothing to add, but only to wish that "the
blessing of many ready to perish, may come upon you.

I am Gentlemen,
Your Servant,
Jupiter Hammon

To the Public: An Address to the Negroes of the State of
New York

When I am writing to you with a design to say something to you
for your good, and with a view to promote your happiness, I can with
truth and sincerity join with the apostle Paul, when speaking of his own
nation the Jews, and say, "That I have great heaviness and continual
sorrow in my heart for my brethren, my kinsmen according to the flesh."
Yes my dear brethren, when I think of you, which is very often, and of
the poor, despised and miserable state you are in, as to the things of this
world, and when I think of your ignorance and stupidity, and the great
wickedness of the most of you, I am pained to the heart. It is at times,
almost too much for human nature to bear, and I am obliged to turn my
thoughts from the subject or endeavour to still my mind, by considering
that it is permitted thus to be, by that God who governs all things, who
seteth up one and pulleth down another. While I have been thinking
on this subject, I have frequently had great struggles in my own mind,
and have been at a loss to know what to do. I have wanted exceedingly
to say something to you, to call upon you with the tenderness of a
father and friend, and to give you the last, and I may say, dying advice,
of an old man, who wishes our best good in this world, and in the

world to come. But while I have had such desires, a sense of my own ignorance, and unfitness to teach others, has frequently discouraged me from attempting to say any thing to you; yet when I thought of your situation, I could not rest easy. When I was at Hartford in Connecticut, where I lived during the war, I published several pieces which were well received, not only by those of my own colour, but by a number of the white people, who thought they might do good among their servants. This is one consideration, among others, that emboldens me now to publish what I have written to you. Another is, I think you will be more likely to listen to what is said, when you know it comes from a negro, one your own nation and colour, and therefore can have no interest in deceiving you, or in saying any thing to you, but what he really thinks is your interest and duty to comply with. My age, I think, gives me some right to speak to you, and reason to expect you will hearken to my advice. I am now upwards of seventy years old, and cannot expect, though I am well, and able to do almost any kind of business, to live much longer. I have passed the common bounds set for man, and must soon go the way of all the earth. I have had more experience in the world than the most of you, and I have seen a great deal of the vanity, and wickedness of it. I have great reason to be thankful that my lot has been so much better than most slaves have had. I suppose I have had more advantages and privileges than most of you, who are slaves have ever known, and I believe more than many white people have enjoyed, for which I desire to bless God, and pray that he may bless those who have given them to me. I do not, my dear friends, say these things about myself to make you think that I am wiser or better than others; but that you might hearken, without prejudice, to what I have to say to you on the following particulars.

1st. Respecting obedience to masters. Now whether it is right, and lawful, in the Sight of God, for them to make slaves of us or not, I am certain that while we are slaves, it is our duty to obey our masters, in all their lawful commands, and mind them unless we are bid to do that which we know to be sin, or forbidden in God's word. The apostle Paul says, "Servants be obedient to them that are your masters according to the flesh, with fear and trembling in singleness in your heart as unto Christ: Not with eye service, as men pleasers, but as the servants of Christ doing the will of God from the heart: With good will doing service to the Lord, and not to men: Knowing that whatever thing a man doeth the same shall he receive of the Lord, whether he be bond or free."—Here is a plain command of God for us to obey our masters. It may seem hard for us, if we think our masters wrong in holding us slaves, to obey in all things, but who of us dare dispute with God! He has commanded us to obey, and we ought to do it cheerfully, and freely. This should be done by us, not only because God commands, but because our own peace and comfort depend upon it. As we depend upon our masters, for what we eat and drink and wear, and for all our comfortable things in this world, we cannot be happy, unless we please them. This we cannot do without obeying tem freely, without muttering or finding fault. If a servant strives to please his master and studies and takes pains to do it, I believe there are but few masters who would use such a servant cruelly. Good servants frequently make good masters. If your master is really hard, unreasonable and cruel, there is no way so likely for you to convince him of it, as always to obey his commands, and try to serve him, and take care of his interest, and try to promote it all in your power. If you are proud and stubborn and always finding fault, your master will think the fault lies wholly on your side, but if you are humble, and meek, and bear all things patiently, your master may think he is wrong, if he does not, his neighbors will be apt to see it, and will befriend you, and try to alter his conduct. If this does not do, you must cry to him, who has the hearts of all men in his hands, and turneth them as the rivers of waters are turned.

2d: The particular I would mention is honesty and faithfulness, you must suffer me now to deal plainly with you, my dear brethren, for I do not mean to flatter, or omit speaking the truth, whether it is for you or against you. How many of you are there who allow yourselves in stealing from your masters. It is very wicked for you not to take care of your masters goods, but how much worse is it to pilfer and steal from them, whenever you think you shall not be found out. This you must know is very wicked and provoking to God. There are none of you so ignorant, but that you must know that this is wrong. Though you may try to excuse yourselves, by saying that your masters are unjust to you, and though you may try to quiet your consciences in this way, yet if you are honest in owning the truth you must think it is as wicked, and on some accounts more wicked to steal from your masters, than from others.

We cannot certainly, have any excuse either for taking any thing that belongs to our masters without their leave, or for being unfaithful in their business. It is our duty to be faithful, not with eye service as men please. We have no right to stay when we are sent on errands, any longer than to do the business we were sent upon. All the time spent idly, is spent wickedly, and is unfaithfulness to our masters. In these things I must say, that I think many of you are guilty. I know that many of you endeavor to excuse yourselves, and say that you have nothing that you can call your own, and that you are under great temptations to be unfaithful and take from your masters. But this will not do, God will certainly punish you for stealing and for being unfaithful. All that we have to mind is our own duty. If God has put us in bad circumstances that is not our fault and he will not punish us for it. If any are wicked in keeping us so, we cannot help it, they must answer to God for it. Nothing will serve as an excuse to us for not doing our duty. The same God will judge both them and us. Pray then my dear friends, fear to offend in this way, but be faithful to God, to your masters, and to your own souls.

The next thing I would mention, and warn you against, Is profaneness. This you know is forbidden by God. Christ tells us, "swear not at all," and again it is said "thou shalt not take the name of the Lord thy God in vain, for the Lord will not hold him guiltless, that taketh his name in vain." Now though the great God has forbidden it, yet how dreadfully profane are many, and I don't know but I may say the most of you? How common is it to hear you take the terrible and awful name of the great God in vain?—To swear by it, and by Jesus Christ, his Son—How common is it to hear yon wish damnation to your companions, and to your own souls and to sport with in the name of Heaven and Hell, as if there were no such places for you to hope for, or to fear, Oh my friends, be warned to forsake this dreadful sin of profaneness. Pray my dear friends, believe and realize, that there is a God—that he is great and terrible beyond what you can think—that he keeps you in life every moment—and that he can send you to that awful Hell, that you laugh at, in an instant, and confine you there for ever, and that he will certainly do it, if you do not repent. You certainly do not believe, that there is a God, or that there is a Heaven or Hell, or you would never trifle with them. It would make you shudder, if you heard others do it, if you believe them as much, as you believe any thing you see with your bodily eyes.

I have heard some learned and good men say, that the heathen, and all that worshiped false Gods, never spoke lightly or irreverently of their Gods, they never took their names in vain, or jested with those things which they held sacred. Now why should the true God, who made all things, be treated worse in this respect, than those false Gods, that were made of wood and stone, I believe it is because Satan tempts men to do it, He tried to make them love their false Gods, and to speak well of them, but he wishes to have men think lightly of the true God, to take his holy name in vain, and to scoff at, and make a jest of all things that are really good. You may think that Satan has not power to do so much, and have so great influence on the minds of men: But the scripture says, "he goeth about like a roaring Lion, seeking whom he may devour-That he is the prince of the power of the air-and that he rules in the hearts of the children of disobedience,-and that wicked men are led captive by him, to do his will." All those of you who are profane, are serving the Devil. You are doing what he tempts and desires you to do. If you could see him with your bodily eyes, would you like to make an agreement with him, to serve him, and do as he bid you. I believe most of you would be shocked at this, but you may be certain that all of you who allow yourselves in this sin, are as really serving him, and to just as good purpose, as if you met him, and promised to dishonor God, and serve him with all your might. Do you believe this? It is true whether you believe it or not, some of you to excuse yourselves, may plead the example of others, and say that you hear a great many white-people, who know more, than such poor ignorant negroes, as you are, and some who are rich and great gentlemen, swear, and talk profanely; and some of you may say this of your masters, and say no more than is true, but all this is not a sufficient excuse for you. You know that murder is wicked. If you saw your master kill a man, do you suppose this would be any excuse for you, if you should commit the same crime? You must know it would not; nor will your hearing him curse and swear, and take the name of God in vain, or any other man, be he ever so great or rich, excuse you. God is greater than all other beings, and him we are bound to obey. To him we must give an account for every idle word that we speak. He will bring us all, rich and poor, white and black, to his judgment seat. If we are found among those who feared his name, and trembled at his word, we shall be called good and faithful servants. Our slavery will be at an end, and though ever so mean, low, and despited in this world, we shall sit with God in his kingdom as Kings and Priests, and rejoice forever, and ever. Do not then, my dear friends, take God's holy name in vain, or speak profanely in any way. Let not the example of others lead you into the sin, but reverence and fear that great and fearful name, the Lord our God. I might now caution you against other sins to which you are exposed; but as I meant only to mention those you were exposed to, more than others, by your being slaves, I will conclude what I have to say to you, by advising you to become religious, and to make religion the great business of your lives.

Now I acknowledge that liberty is a great thing, and worth seeking for, if we can get it honestly, and by our good conduct, prevail on our masters to set us free: Though for my own part I do not wish to be free, yet I should be glad, if others, especially the young negroes were to be free, for many of us, who are grown up slaves, and have always had masters to take care of us, should hardly know how to take care of ourselves; and it may be more for our own comfort to remain as we are. That liberty is a great thing we may know from our own feelings, and we may likewise Judge so from the conduct of the white-people, in the late war. How much money has been spent, and how many lives has been lost, to defend their liberty. I must say that I have hoped that God would open their eyes, when they were so much engaged for liberty, to think of the state of the poor blacks, and to pity us. He has done it in some measure, and has raised us up many friends, for which we have reason to be thankful, and to hope in his mercy. What may be done further, he only knows, for known unto God are all his ways from the beginning. But this my dear brethren Is by no means, the greatest thing we have to be concerned about. Getting our liberty in this world, is nothing to our having the liberty of the children of God. Now the Bible tells us that we are all by nature, sinners, that we are slaves to sin and Satan, and that unless we are converted, or born again, we must be miserable forever. Christ says, except a man be born again, he cannot see the kingdom of God, and all that do not see the kingdom of God, must be in the kingdom of darkness.

There are but two places where all go after death, white and black, rich and poor; those places are Heaven and Hell. Heaven is a place made for those, who are born again, and who love God, and it is a place where they will be happy for ever. Hell Is a place made for those who hate God, and are his enemies, and where they will be miserable to all eternity. Now you may think you are not enemies to God, and do not hate him: But if your heart has not been changed, and you have not become true Christians, you certainly are enemies to God, and have been opposed to him ever since you were born. Many of you, I suppose, never think of this, and are almost as ignorant as the beasts that perish. Those of you who can read I must beg you to read the Bible, and whenever you can get time, study the Bible, and if you can get no other time, spare some of your time from sleep, and learn what the mind and will of God is. But what shall I say to them who cannot read. This lay with great weight on my mind, when I thought of writing to my poor brethren, but I hope that those who can read will take pity on them and read what I have to say to them. In hopes of this I will beg of you to spare no pains in trying to learn to read. If you are once engaged you may learn. Let all the time you can get be spent in trying to learn to read. Get those who can read to learn you, but remember, that what you learn for, is to read the Bible. If there was no Bible, it would be no matter whether you could read or not. Reading other books would do you no good. But the Bible is the word of God, and tells you what you must do to please God; it tells you how you may escape misery, and be happy for ever. If you see most people neglect the Bible, and many that can read never look into it, let it not harden you and make you think lightly of it, and that it is a book of no worth. All those who are really good, love the Bible, and meditate on it day and night. In the Bible God has told us every thing it is necessary we should know, in order to be happy here and hereafter. The Bible is a revelation of the mind and will of God to men. Therein we may learn, what God is. That he made all things by the power of his word; and that he made all things for his own glory, and not for our glory. That he is over all, and above all his creatures, and more above them that we can think or conceive-that they can do nothing without him-that he upholds them all, and will over-rule all things for his own glory. In the Bible likewise we are told what man is. That he was at first made holy, in the image of God, that he fell from that state of holiness, and became an enemy to God, and that since the fall, all the imaginations of the thoughts of his heart, are evil and only evil, and that continually. That the carnal mind is not subject to the law of God, neither indeed can be. And that all mankind, were under the wrath, and curse of God, and must have been for ever miserable, if they had been left to suffer what their sins deserved. It tells us that God, to save some of mankind, sent his Son into this world to die, in the room and stead of sinners, and that now God can save from eternal misery, all that believe in his Son, and take him for their saviour, and that all are called upon to repent, and believe in Jesus Christ. It tells us that those who do repent, and believe, and are friends to Christ, shall have many trials and sufferings in this world, but that they shall be happy forever, after death, and reign with Christ to all eternity. The

Bible tells us that this world is a place of trial, and that there is no other time or place for us to alter, but in this life. If we are Christians when we die, we shall awake to the resurrection of life; if not, we shall awake to the resurrection of damnation. It tells us, we must all live in Heaven or Hell, be happy or miserable, and that without end. The Bible does not tell us of but two places, for all to go to. There is no place for innocent folks, that are not Christians. There is no place for ignorant folks, that did not know how to be Christians. What I mean is, that there is no place besides Heaven and Hell. These two places, will receive all mankind, for Christ says, there are but two sorts, he that is not with me is against me, and he that gathereth not with me, scattereth abroad.- The Bible likewise tells us that this world, and all things in it shall be burnt up-and that "God has appointed a day in which he will judge the world, and that he will bring every secret thing whether it be good or bad into judgment that which is done in secret shall be declared on the house top." I do not know, nor do I think any can tell, but that the day of judgment may last a thousand years. God could tell the state of all his creatures in a moment, but then every thing that every one has done, through his whole life is to be told, before the whole world of angels, and men. There, Oh how solemn is the thought! You, and I, must stand, and hear every thing we have thought or done, however secret, however wicked and vile, told before all the men and women that ever have been, or ever will be, and before all the angels, good and bad.

Now my dear friends seeing the Bible is the word of God, and every thing in it is true, and it reveals such awful and glorious things, what can be more important than that you should learn to read it; and when you have learned to read, that you should study it day and night. There are some things very encouraging in God's word for such ignorant creatures as we are; for God hath not chosen the rich of this world. Not many rich, not many noble are called, but God hath chosen the weak things of this world, and things which are not, to confound the things that are: And when the great and the rich refused coming to the gospel feast, the servant was told, to go into the highways, and hedges, and compel those poor creatures that he found there to come in. Now my brethren it seems to me, that there are no people that ought to attend to the hope of happiness in another world so much as we do. Most of us are cut off from comfort and happiness here in this world, and can expect nothing from It. Now seeing this is the case, why should we not take care to be happy after death. Why should we spend our whole lives in sinning against God: And be miserable in this world, and in the world to come. If we do thus, we shall certainly be the greatest fools. We shall be slaves here, and slaves forever. We cannot plead so great temptations to neglect religion as others. Riches and honours which drown the greater part of mankind, who have the gospel, in perdition, can be little or no temptations to us.

We live so little time in this world that it is no matter how wretched and miserable we are, if it prepares us for heaven. What is forty, fifty, or sixty years, when compared to eternity. When thousands and millions of years have rolled away, this eternity will be no nigher coming to an end. Oh how glorious is an eternal life of happiness! And how dreadful, an eternity of misery. Those of us who have had religious masters, and have been taught to read the Bible, and have been brought by their example and teaching to a sense of divine things, how happy shall we be to meet them in heaven, where we shall join them in praising God forever. But if any of us have had such masters, and yet have lived and died wicked, how will it add to our misery to think of Our folly. If any of us, who have wicked and profane masters should become religious, how will our estates be changed in another world. Oh my friends, let me entreat of you to think on these things, and to live as if you believed them to be true. If you become Christians you will have reason to bless God forever, that you have been brought into a land where you have heard the gospel, though you have been slaves. If we should ever get to Heaven, we shall find nobody to reproach us for being black, or for being slaves. Let me beg of you my dear African brethren, to think very little of your bondage in this life, for your thinking of it will do you no good. If God designs to set us free, he will do it, in his own time, and way; but think of your bondage to sin and Satan, and do not rest, until you are delivered from it. We cannot be happy if we are ever so free or ever so rich, while we are servants of sin, and slaves to Satan. We must be miserable here, and to all eternity. I will conclude what I have to say with a few words to those negroes who have their liberty. The most of what I have said to those who are slaves may be of use to you, but you have more advantages, on some accounts, if you will improve your freedom, as you may do, than they. You have more time to read God's holy word, and to take care of the salvation of your souls. Let me beg of you to spend your time in this way, or it will be better for you, if you had always been slaves. If you think seriously of the matter, you must conclude, that if you do not use your freedom, to promote the salvation of your souls, it will not be of any lasting good to you. Besides all this, if you are idle, and take to bad courses, you will hurt those of your brethren who are slaves, and do all in your power to prevent their being free. Our great reason that is given by some for not freeing us, I understand is, that we should not know how to take care of ourselves, and should take to bad courses. That we should be lazy and idle, and get drunk and steal. Now all those of you, who follow any bad courses, and who do not take care to get an honest living by your labour and industry, are doing more to prevent our being free, than any body else. Let me beg of you then for the sake of your own good and happiness, in time, and for eternity, and for the sake of your poor brethren, who are still in bondage "to lead quiet and peaceable lives in all Godliness and honesty," and may God bless you, and bring yo to his kingdom, for Christ's sake, Amen.

An Evening's Improvement: Shewing, the Necessity of Beholding the Lamb of God

Behold the Lamb of God which taketh away the sins of the world.

—*John I.29*

In the beginning of this chapter John bears testimony, that Jesus is the Son of God. Verse 1st. In the beginning was the word, and the word was with God, and the word was God. This is that Lamb of God which I now invite you to behold. My Brethren, we are to behold the Son of God as our Lord and giver of life for he was made flesh and dwelt among us, verse 14 of the context, and here he is declared to be the Son of God full of grace and truth. And here in the first place I mean to shew the necessity of beholding the Lamb of God in the sense of the text. 2d. Endeavour to shew when we are said to behold the Son of God in the sense of the text. 3d. I shall shew when we may be said not to behold the Lamb of God as we should do. In the 4th place I shall endeavor to shew how far we may be mistaken in beholding the Lamb of God. In the 5th place I shall endeavor to rectify these mistakes.

My brethren, since I wrote my Winter Piece it hath been requested that I would write something more for the advantage of my friends, by my superiors, gentlemen, whose judgment I depend on, and by my friends in general, I have had an invitation to give a public exhortation; but did not think it my duty at that time; but now, my brethren, by divine assistance, I shall endeavor to shew the necessity of beholding the Lamb of God. My brethren we must behold the Lamb of God as taking away the sin of the world, as in our text, and it is necessary that we behold the Lamb of God as our King: ah! as the King immortal, eternal, invisible, as the only Son of God, for he hath declared him, as in the 8th verse of the context, no man hath seen God at any time: The only begotten Son, which is in the bosom of the Father, he hath declared him. My brethren, let us strive to behold the Lamb of God, with faith and repentance; to come weary and heavy laden with our sin, for they have made us unworthy of the mercy of the Lamb of God; therefore, we see how necessary it is that we behold the Lamb of God, in the sense of the text, that is, in a spritual manner, not having on our own righteousness; but we must be cloathed upon, with the unspotted robes of the Lamb of God; we must work out our salvation with fear and trembling, always abounding in the works of the Lord; we must remember the vows of our baptism, which is to follow the Lamb of God, John Chap. I.33. speaking of baptism, he saith, upon whom thou shalt see the spirit descending and remaining on him, the same is he which baptiseth with the Holy Ghost, and verse 34, and I saw, and bare record, that this is the Son of God, verse 35, again the next day after, John stood and two of his disciples, verse 36, and looking upon Jesus, as he walked, and saith, behold the Lamb of God, verse 37, and the two disciples heard him speak and they followed Jesus. Thus, my dear brethren, we are to follow the Lamb of God, at all times, whether in prosperity or adversity, knowing that all things work together for good, to them that love God, or as in Rom. viii.28. now let us manifest that we love God, by a holy life; let us strive to glorify and magnify the name of the most high God. It is necessary that we behold the Lamb of God, by taking heed to our ways, that we sin not with our tongues, Psalm xxxix.1. Here, my brethren, we have the exhortation of David, who beheld the Lamb of God with faith and love, for he crys out with a most humble petition, O Lord, rebuke me not in thine anger; neither chastise me in thy hot displeasure. Psalm vi.1. and now, my brethren, have we not great reason to cry to the Lamb of God, that taketh away the sin of the world, that he may have mercy on us and forgive us our sins, and that he would give us his holy spirit, that we may have such hungerings and thirsting as may be acceptable in the sight of God, for as the heart panteth for the water brook, so should our souls pant for the living God. Psalm xlii.1. and now, my brethren, we must behold the law of God, as is exprest, John I.51.

And he saith unto him, verily, verily I say unto you, hereafter you shall see heaven open, and the angels of God ascending and descending upon the Son of man. This is a representation of the great day, when the Lamb of God shall appear. Matt. xxiv.30, and then shall appear the sign of the Son of Man in heaven, and then shall the tribes of the earth mourn, and they shall see the Son of Man coming in the clouds of heaven, with power and great glory. Here my brethren, we have life and death set before us, for if we mourn with the tribes for our sins, which have made us unworthy of the least favour in the sight of God, then he will have mercy and he will give us his holy spirit; then we shall have hearts to pray to the Lamb of God, as David did when he was made sensible of his imperfections, then he cryed to the Lamb of

God, have mercy upon me O God, Psal. lxi.1, according to thy loving kindness, according to the multitude of thy tender mercies, blot out my transgressions. This my brethren is the language of the penitent, for he hath a desire that his heart may be turned from darkness to light, from sin to holiness; this none can do but God; for the carnal mind is enmity against God, for it is not subject to the law of God, neither can be. Here we see that we must behold the Lamb of God as calling to us in the most tender and compassionate manner, Matt. xxiii.37, saying, O Jerusalem, Jerusalem, how often would I have gathered thy children together, even as a hen gathereth her chickens under her wings, and ye would not. As much as if he had said, O ye wicked and rebellious people have I not given my word as a rule of life; have I not sent the ministers of the gospel to teach you, and you will not receive the doctrine of the gospel, which is faith and repentance, I tell you nay; but except ye repent ye shall all likewise perish, Luke xiii.4.

And now my dear brethren, have we repented of our sins? Have we not neglected to attend divine service? Or if we have attended to the word of God, have we been sincere? For God is a spirit, and they that worship him must worship him in spirit and truth, John iv.24. When we have heard the word of God sounding in our ears, inviting of us to behold the Lamb of God; O my dear brethren, have we as it were laid up these words in our hearts, or have we not been like the stony ground hearers? Matt. xii.20. But he that received the seed into stony places, the same is he that heareth the word, and anon with joy receiveth it. Ver. 21. Yet hath not root in himself, but dureth for a while; for when tribulation or persecution ariseth because of the word, by and by he is offended. This is the effect of a hard heart. There is such a depravity in our natures that we are not willing to suffer any reproach that may be cast on us for the sake of our religion; this my brethren is because we have not the love of God shed abroad in our hearts; but our hearts are set too much on the pleasures of this life, forgetting that they are passing away; but the children of God are led by the spirit of God. Rom. viii.12, Therefore brethren we are debtors, not to the flesh to live after the flesh. Ver. 13, For if ye live after the flesh ye shall die; but if through the spirit do mortify the deeds of the body, ye shall live. Ver. 14, For as many are led by the spirit of God, they are the sons of God. Here my brethren we see that it is our indispensible duty to conform to the will of God in all things, not having our hearts set on the pleasures of this life; but we must prepare for death, our great and last change. For we are sinners by nature, and are adding thereunto by evil practices; for man is prone to evil as the sparks to fly upward; and there is nothing short of the divine power of the most high God can turn our hearts to see the living and true God; and now we ought to behold the Lamb of God, as it is expressed in Isaiah vii.14, A virgin shall conceive and bear a son, and shall call his name Emanuel. This my brethren is the Son of God, who died to save us guilty sinners, and it is only by the mercy of the blessed Jesus we can be saved: Therefore, let us cast off self-dependence, and rely on a crucified Saviour, whose blood was shed for all that came unto him by faith and repentance; this we cannot do of ourselves, but we must be found in the use means; therefore we ought to come as David did, Psal. li.1. Have mercy on me O God, according to thy loving kindness.

This my brethren is the duty of all flesh to come to the divine fountain, and to confess our sins before the most high God; for if we say we have no sin we deceive ourselves and the truth is not in us; but if we confess our sins he is faithful and just to forgive us our transgressions. And now my brethren, seeing I have had an invitation to write something more to encourage my dear fellow servants and brethren, Africans, in the knowledge of the Christian religion, I must beg your patience, for I mean to use the utmost brevity that so important a subject will admit of; and now my brethren, we have, as I observed in the foregoing part of this discourse, life and death set before us, for we are invited to come and accept of Christ on the terms of the gospel. Isaiah xliv.1, O every one that thirsteth, come ye to the waters, and he that hath no money, come ye buy and eat, yea, come ye buy wine and milk, without money and without price. Here is life, and if we search our hearts, and try our ways, and turn again unto the Lord he will forgive us our sins and blot out our transgressions, Lamen. iii.40. But if we continue in our sins, having our hearts set on the pleasures of this life, forgetting that we must give an account for the deeds done in the body. Psal. lxii.12, Also unto the Lord belongeth mercy, for he rendereth to every man according to his works. Here we see that we should behold the Lamb of God by a holy life. Psal. vii.11, God judgeth the righteous and is angry with the wicked every day, ver. 12, if he turn not. He will whet his sword, he hath bent his bow and made it ready. Here we see that the wrath of God abideth on the unbelievers and unconverted sinner. And now my brethren, should not a sense of these things make us cry out in the apostle's language, "Men and brethren what shall we do to be saved?" We must be found in the use of means, and pray that God would be pleased to rain down a rain of righteousness into our souls; then we shall behold the Lamb of God as taking away the sins of the world. Let us my brethren examine ourselves whether we have had a saving change wrought in our hearts, and have been brought to bow to the divine sovereignty of a crucified Saviour; have we been brought to behold the Lamb of God, by obeying the precepts of Isaiah, and turning from evil and learning to do well. Isaiah i.16, Wash ye, make you clean; put away the evil of your doing from before mine eyes; cease to do evil, learn to do well. Here we have the admonition of the prophet Isaiah, who was inspired with the knowledge of divine things, so that he calls heaven and earth to witness against the wicked and rebellious sinner. Isaiah i.2, Here O heavens and give ear O earth; for the Lord hath spoken, I have nourished up children, and they have rebelled against me. Is not this the case? Have we not been going astray like lost sheep? Luke xv.6, Have we not great reason to lay our hands on our mouths and our mouths in the dust, and come upon the bended knees of our souls and beg for mercy as the publican did, saying, God be merciful to me a sinner, Luke viii.13. This my dear brethren should be the language of our conversation; to have a life void of offence towards God and towards man. Have we beheld the Lamb of God, by taking up our cross, denying ourselves, and following the blessed Jesus. Matt. xvi.24, Then said Jesus unto his disciples, if any man will be my disciple, let him deny himself, take up his cross and follow me. Here we see that we should behold the Lamb of God as our only Saviour and mighty Redeemer, and we are to take up our cross and follow the Lamb of God at all times, not to murmur at the hand of Divine Providence; and we have our example set before us, Luke xxii.41, 42, And he was withdrawn from them about a stone's cast, and he kneeled down and prayed, saying, my Father, if thou be willing, remove this cup from me, nevertheless not my will but thine be done. We should behold the Lamb of God as coming in the clouds of heaven with great power and glory, whom our heavenly Father hath declared to be his only Son. Matt. xvii.5, And while he yet spoke, behold a bright cloud overshadowed them; and behold a voice out of the cloud which said, this is my beloved Son in whom I am well pleased, hear him. Should not a sense of these things inflame our hearts with fear and love to God; knowing that there is no other name given by which we can be saved, but by the name of Jesus; let us behold the Lamb of God as having power to make the blind to see, the dumb to speak, and the lame to walk, and even to raise the dead: But it may be objected and said by those that have had the advantage of studying, are we to expect miracles at this day? These things were done to confirm that Jesus was the Son of God, and to free us from the burthen of types and ceremonies of the Jewish law; and this by way of instruction, which I desire to receive with an humble spirit. Others may object and say, what can we expect from an unlearned Ethiopian? And this by way of reflection. To this I answer, Pray Sir, give me leave to ask this question, Doth not the raising of Lazarus give us a sight of our sinful natures? John xi.12, 13, And when he had thus spoken, he said with a loud voice, Lazarus come forth. Ver. 4, And he that was dead came forth, bound hand and foot with grave clothes, and his head was bound with a napkin; Jesus saith unto them, loose him and let him go. Is not this a simile of our deadness by nature? And there is nothing short of the power of the most high God can raise us to life. Sirs, I know we are not to expect miracles at this day; but hear the words of our Saviour Matt. xvi.16, And Simon Peter answered and said, thou art Christ the Son of the living God. Ver. 17, And Jesus answered and said unto him, blessed art thou Simon Barjona, for flesh and blood hath not revealed it unto thee, but my Father which is in heaven. Sirs, this may suffice to prove that it is by grace we are saved, and that not of ourselves, is the gift of God. But my brethren, for whom this discourse is designed, I am now in the second place to shew when we are said to behold the Lamb of God in the sense of the text: When we are brought humbly to confess our sins, before the most high God, and are calling on our souls and all that is within us to bless his holy name; this is the duty of all flesh, to praise God for his unmerited mercy in giving his Son to save lost man, who by the fall of Adam became guilty in the sight of God. Rom. v.8, But God commandeth his love towards us, in that while we were sinners Christ died for us. Here we are to behold the Lamb of God as suffering for our sins, and it is only by the precious blood of Christ we can be saved, when we are made sensible of our own imperfections and are desirous to love and fear God; this we cannot do of ourselves, for this is the work of God's holy spirit. John vi.64, And he said, therefore said I unto you that no man can come unto me except it were given unto him of my Father. Here we see to behold the Lamb of God, in the sense of the text, as the gift of God; we should come as David did, saying, O Lord rebuke me not in thine anger, neither chastise me in thy hot displeasure, Psal. v.1. And we should put our whole trust in the Lord at all times; we should strive to live a religious life, to avoid the very appearance of evil, least we incur the wrath of God. Psal. xi.6, Upon the wicked he shall rain showers of fire and brimstone, and an horrible tempest; this shall be the portion of their cup. Here we see the unhappy state of the sinner; for he is not only led away by that subtle adversary the devil, but he hath the word of God pronounced against him. Matt. xxv.40, Then shall he say unto them on the left hand depart from me ye cursed into everlasting fire prepared for the devil and his angels. Here my brethren we are to behold the Lamb of God as being crucified for us. Matt. xxiii.20, Pilate therefore willing to release Jesus spake again to them. ver. 22, But they cryed, saying crucify him, crucify him. Here we see the effect of sin; the blood of Christ was shed for all that came unto him by faith and repentance. O my brethren, when those things have a proper influence on our minds, by the power of the most high God, to say as David did, Psal. ciii.1, Bless the Lord O my soul, and forget not all his benefits. Then we may be said to behold the Lamb of God in the sense of the text: And we are to behold the Lamb of God as it is expressed in Matt. xvii.22, And while they abode in Galilee Jesus said unto them, the Son of Man shall be betrayed into the hands of men; and ver. 23, And they shall kill him, and the third day he shall rise again. And now should not a sense of these things have a tendency to make us humble in the sight of God, and we should see the place and situation of Christ suffering. Luke xxii.33, And when they were come to the place called Calvary, there they crucified him, and the malefactors one on the right hand and the other on the left. Here we see the boundless riches of free grace; he is numbered with transgressors, whose blood speaks better things than the blood of Abel; for the blood of Abel calls for justice on the sinner, but the blood of Christ calls for mercy. Luke xxiii.34, Then said Jesus, Father forgive them, for they know not what they do. Here we have the example of our Saviour, that we should forgive our enemies, and pray that God would forgive them also, or how shall we say the Lord's Prayer, "Forgive us our tresspasses as we forgive them that trespass against us." Now when we are enabled to do these things, as we should do them, then may we be said to behold the Lamb of God in the sense of the text. And now my dear brethren, I am to remind you of a most melancholy scene of Providence; it hath pleased the most high God, in his wise providence, to permit a cruel and unnatural war to be commenced; let us examine ourselves whether we have not been the cause of this heavy judgment;

have we been truly thankful for mercies bestowed? And have we been humbled by afflictions? For neither mercies nor afflictions proceed from the dust, but they are the works of our heavenly Father; for it may be that when the tender mercies of God will not allure us, afflictions may drive us to the divine fountain. Let us now cast an eye back for a few years and consider how many hundreds of our nation and how many thousands of other nations have been sent out of time into a never-ending eternity, by the force of the cannon and by the point of the sword. Have we not great cause to think this is the just deserving of our sins; for this is the word of God. Isaiah iii.11, Wo unto the wicked, it shall be ill with him, for the reward of his hands shall be given him. Here we see that we ought to pray, that God may hasten the time when the people shall beat their swords into plough-shares and their spears into pruning hooks, and nations shall learn war no more.

And now my dear brethren have we not great reason to be thankful that God in the time of his judgments hath remembered mercy, so that we have the preaching of the gospel and the use of our bibles, which is the greatest of all mercies; and if after all these advantages we continue in our sins, have we not the greatest reason to fear the judgments of God will be fulfilled on us. He that being often reproved hardneth his neck shall suddenly be destroyed, and that without remedy. Have we not great reason to praise God that he is giving us food and raiment, and to say as David did, Psal. cxxxvii.1, O give thanks unto the Lord, for his mercy endureth forever. And now my brethren, when these things make us more humble and more holy, then we may be said to behold the Lamb of God in the sense of the text. And now, in the third place, I am to shew when we may be said not to behold the Lamb of God in the sense of the text: When we are negligent to attend the word of God, and unnecessarily, or are living in any known sin, either of omission or commission, or when we have heard the word peached to us and have not improved that talent put into our hands by a holy life, then we may be said not to behold the Lamb of God in the sense of the text. And now my brethren, I am in the fourth place, to shew how in some things we may be mistaken in beholding the Lamb of God, while we are flattering ourselves with the hopes of salvation on the most slight foundation, because we live in a Christian land and attend to divine service; these things are good in themselves; but there must be a saving change wrought in our hearts, and we must become a new in Christ

Jesus; we must not live after the flesh, but after the spirit, for as many as are led by the spirit of God are the sons of God, Rom. viii.14. and we are to pray that God would keep us from all evil, especially the evil of sin. Bishop Bevrage, in his second Resolution, speaking of sin, he says, "For as God is the centre of all good, so sin is the fountain of all evil in the world, all strife and contention, ignominy and disgrace." Read a little further, and he goes on to protest against sin, "I resolve to hate sin (says he) wherever I find it, whether in myself or in others, in the best of my friends as well as in the worst of my enemies." Here we see my brethren that if we commit any willful sin, either of omission or commission, we become the servants of sin, and are deceiving ourselves, for the apostle hath told us, that the wages of sin is death, Rom. vi.22, 23; but now being made free from sin, and are become the servants of God ye have your fruits into holiness, and in the end eternal life; for the wages of sin is death, but the gift of God is eternal life through Jesus Christ our Lord We are to behold the Lamb of God by reading the scriptures, and we must believe that he hath power to give everlasting life. John vi.47, Verily, verily I say unto you, he that believeth on me hath everlasting life. Do we my brethren believe in the blessed Jesus as we ought? Are we not going the broad way to utter destruction? Are we not leaving the blessed Jesus, who hath the bread of life and is that bread? John vi.48, I am the bread of life. Here we see that the blessed Jesus hath power to give eternal life to all that come unto him by faith and repentance; and we see that he is calling to us as he did to his disciples, saying, Wilt thou go away also; for this is the language of the scriptures, John vi.67, 68, Then Simon answered him, Lord to whom shall we go? Thou hast the words of eternal life. And we are my brethren to behold the Lamb of God as being the door of eternal life, for this he hath declared in his word to us. John x.9, I am the door, by me if any man enter he shall be saved, and shall go in and out and find pasture.

But it is very plain my brethren that if we come in our sins God will not hear us, but if we come and worship him in spirit and in truth he will have mercy on us. John ix.31, 32, Now we know that God heareth not sinners, but if any man be a worshipper of God and doth his will, him he neareth. My dear brethren as I am drawing to a conclusion, let me press on you to prepare for death, that great and irresistable king of terrors, by a holy life, and make the word of God the rule of your life; but it may be objected we do not understand the word of God. Mr. Burkit, a great divine of our church says, in the scriptures there is depths that an elephant may swim, and shoals that a lamb may wade. Therefore we must take the plainest text as a key to us. And now my brethren I am in the fifth place to endeavour to rectify any mistake we may labour under, when we are taking on us the form of Godliness, without the power thereof, then we cannot be said to behold the Lamb of God in the sense of the text. We must pray earnestly to God for his holy Spirit to guide us in the way to eternal life; this none can do but God. Let us my brethren lay up treasure in heaven, where neither moth doth corrupt nor thieves break through and steal. Matt. vi.20–23, Seek first the kingdom of God and his righteousness and all these things shall be added unto you. And now my dear brethren, we must pray earnestly to God for the influence of his holy spirit to guide us through this howling wilderness and sea of trouble to the mansions of glory, and we should pray that God would give us grace to love and to fear him, for if we love God, black as we be, and despised as we are, God will love us. Acts x.34, Then Peter opened his mouth and said, of a truth I perceive that God has no respect to persons. Ver. 35, In every nation he that feareth him is accepted of him. Psalm. xxxiv.8, O taste and see that the Lord is good, and blessed is the man that trusteth in him. Ver. 15, The eyes of the Lord are upon the righteous, and his ears are open to their cry. Let us my dear brethren remember that the time is hastening when we shall appear before the Lamb of God to give an account for the deeds done in the body, when we shall be stumbling over the dark mountains of death looking into an endless eternity. O that we may be of that happy number that shall stand with their lamps burning. Matt. xxv.7, Then all those virgins rose and trimmed their lamps. Come now my brethren, let us examine ourselves whether we have had a saving change wrought in our hearts, and have been brought to bow to the divine sovereignty of the most high God, and to flee to the armies of Jesus, for he is the author of our peace, and the finisher of our faith. Heb. xii.2, Looking to Jesus the author and finisher of our faith. Come now my brethren, we are one flesh and bone, let us serve the one living and true God. Come let us behold the Lamb of God by an eye of faith, for without faith it is impossible to please God. Heb. xi.5, For faith my brethren is of the things not seen. Let us my brethren strive by the grace of God to become new creatures; for if any man be in Christ he is a new creature, 2. Cor. iv.17. Let us come to the divine fountain, by constant prayer. Psal. iv.1, Give ear to my words O Lord, consider my meditations, ver. 2, 3. Let us improve our talents by a holy life, striving to make our calling and election sure, for now is the accepted time; behold now is the day of salvation. 2. Cor. vi.2.

Let us pray that God give us of the waters that the woman of Samaria drank. John xiv.19, But whosoever shall drink of the water I shall give him shall never thirst, but the water I shall give him shall be in him a well of water springing up into everlasting life. O my dear brethren we should be brought humbly to submit to the will of God at all times, and to say God be merciful to us sinners. Acts iii.19, Repent and be converted that your sins may be blotted out. My dear brethren we are many of us seeking for a temporal freedom, and I pray that God would grant your desire; if we are slaves it is by the permission of God; if we are free it must be by the power of the most high God; be not discouraged, but cheerfully perform the duties of the day, sensible that the same power that created the heavens and the earth and causeth the greater light to rule the day and the lesser to rule the night, can cause a universal freedom; and I pray God may give you grace to seek that freedom which tendeth to everlasting life. John viii.32, And ye shall know the truth, and the truth shall make you free. Ver. 36, If the Son shall make you free, then you shall be free indeed. But as I am advanced to the age of seventy-one years, I do not desire temporal freedom for myself. My brethren, if we desire to be a happy people, we must be a holy people, and endeavour to keep the commandments of God, and we should pray that God would come and knock at the door of our hearts by the power of his holy spirit, and give us a stedfastness in the merits of Christ, and we are to believe in Christ for eternal salvation. Mr. Stoddard, a great divine, says, in speaking of appearing in the righteousness of Christ, when men believe it is part of God's covenant, to make them continue to believe. Job. vi.12. And again he saith, since God hath promised life unto all that believe in this righteousness, it must needs be safe to appear before God in this righteousness. Jer. iii.22, Return ye back-sliding children and I will heal your back-slidings; behold we come unto thee for thou art the Lord our God.

My dear brethren let not your hearts be set too much on the pleasures of this life; for if it were possible for one man to gain a thousand freedoms, and had not an interest in the merits of Christ, where must all the advantage be; for what would it profit a man if he should gain the whole world and loose his own soul, Matt. xvi.26. My brethren we know not how soon God may send the cold hand of death to summon us out of this life to a never-ending eternity, there to appear before the judgment seat of Christ. 2 Cor. v.10, For all must appear before the judgment seat of Christ. And now I conclude with a few words—let me tell you my dear brethren, that in a few days we must all appear before the judgment seat of Christ, there to give an account for the deeds done in the body. Let us my brethren strive to be so prepared for death, by the grace of God, that when the time shall come when we are shaking off the shackles of this life, and are passing through the valley of the shadow of death. O may we then be enabled to say, come Lord Jesus come quickly, for thou art the Lamb of God, in whom my soul delighteth: Then my dear brethren all those which have repented of their sins shall hear this voice, come unto me. Matt. xxv.34, Then shall the King say unto them on his right hand; come ye blessed of my Father, inherit the kingdom prepared for you from the foundation of the world. But if we do not repent of our sins we must hear this voice, Matt. xxv.41, Then shall he say also unto them on his left hand, depart from me ye cursed into everlasting fire prepared for the devil and his angels. Then will our souls waft away into an endless eternity, and our bodies lodged in the cold and silent grave, there to remain till Christ's second coming. My brethren, we believe the word of God, we must believe this. 1 Cor. xiii.41, Behold I shew you a mistery, we shall not all sleep, but we shall be changed in a moment in the twinkling of an eye, at the last trumpet; for the trumpet shall sound and the dead shall be raised, ver. 35, For this corruptable must put on incorruption, and this mortals must put on immortality. And now my brethren, let me persuade you to seek the Lord. Isaiah lv.6, Seek the Lord while he may be found, and call on him while he is near; ver. 7, Let the wicked forsake his way, and the unrighteous man his thoughts, and let him return unto the Lord, and he will have mercy on him, and to our God and he will abundantly pardon. Therefore not be contented with the form of godliness without the power thereof. AMEN.

A Winter Piece: Being a Serious Exhortation, with a Call to the Unconverted: And a Short Contemplation on the Death of Jesus Christ

As I have been desired to write something more than Poetry, I shall endeavour to write from these words, Matthew xi, 28. *Come unto me all ye that labour and are heavy laden.*

My Brethren, I shall endeavour by divine assistance, to shew what is meant by coming to the Lord Jesus Christ labouring and heavy laden, and to conclude, I shall contemplate on the death of Jesus Christ.

My Brethren, in the first place, I am to shew what is meant by coming to Christ labouring and heavy laden. We are to come with a sense of our own unworthiness, and to confess our sins before the most high God, and to come by prayer and meditation, and we are to confess Christ to be our Saviour and mighty Redeemer. Matthew x, 33. *Whosoever shall confess me before men, him will I confess before my heavenly father.* Here, my brethren, we have great encouragement to come to the Lord, and ask for the influence of his holy spirit, and that he would give us the water of eternal life, John iv. 14. Whosoever shall drink of this water as the woman of Samaria did, shall never thirst; but it shall be in them a well of water springing up to eternal life, then we shall believe in the merits of Christ, for our eternal salvation, and come labouring and heavy laden with a sense of our lost and undone state without an interest in the merits of Christ. It should be our greatest care to trust in the Lord, as David did, Psalm xxxi, 1. *In thee O Lord put I my trust.*

My Brethren, we must come to the divine fountain to turn us from sin to holiness, and to give us grace to repent of all our sins; this none can do but God. We must come labouring and heavy laden not trusting to our own righteousness, but we are to be cloathed with the righteousness of Christ. Then may we apply this text, Psalm xxxiii, 7. *Blessed is he whose transgressions is forgiven, whose sins is covered.* This we must seek for by prayer and meditation, and we are to pray without ceasing, and the word is set forth by David in Psalm lxi, 1. *Have mercy on me O God, according to thy loving kindness, according unto the multitude of thy tender mercies blot out my transgressions.* My Brethren we are to come poor in spirit.

In the second place in order to come to the divine fountain labouring and heavy laden, we are to avoid all bad company, to keep ourselves pure in heart.

Matthew v. 8. *Blessed are the poor in heart for they shall see God.* Now, in order to see God we must have a saving change wrought in our hearts, which is the work of God's holy spirit which we are to ask for, Matthew vii, 7. *Ask and it shall be given you, seek and ye shall find.* It may be asked what shall we find? Ye will find the mercies of God to allure you, the influence of his holy spirit to guide you in the right way to eternal life, Matt. vii, 8. *For every one that asketh receiveth,* but then my brethren we are to ask in a right manner, with faith and repentance, for except we repent we shall surely die, that is, we must suffer the wrath of the most high God, who will turn you away with this pronunciation *depart from me ye workers of iniquity,* Matt. vii, 23. Therefore you see how dangerous a thing it is to live in any known sin, either of commission or omission, for if we commit any wilful sin, we become the servants of sin.

John viii, 34. *Whosoever commiteth sin is the servant of sin.* My dear brethren, have we not rendered ourselves too much the servants of sin, by a breach of God's holy commandments, by breaking his holy Sabbath, when we should have been fitting for our great and last change? Have we not been amusing ourselves with the pleasures of this life, or, if we have attended divine service, have we been sincere? For God will not be mocked, for he knows our thoughts. John iv, 24, *God is a spirit, and they that worship him must worship him in spirit and in truth.* Therefore my Brethren, we see how necessary it is that we should be sincere when we attempt to come to the Lord whether in public service or private devotion, for it is not the outward appearance but sincerity of the heart. This we must manifest by a holy life; for it is not every one that says Lord, Lord, shall enter into the kingdom of Heaven; but he that doth the will of my heavenly Father, Matt. vii, 21.

Therefore, we ought to come labouring and heavy laden to the throne of grace and pray that God may be pleased to transform us anew in Christ Jesus. But it may be objected by those who have had the advantage of studying, every one is not calculated for teaching of others. To those I answer, Sirs, I do not attempt to teach those who I know are able to teach me, but I shall endeavour by divine assistance to enlighten the minds of my brethren; for we are a poor despised nation, whom God in his wise providence has permitted to be brought from their native place to a Christian land, and many thousands born in what are called Christian families, and brought up to years of understanding. In answer to the objectors, Sirs, pray give me leave to enquire into the state of those children that are born in those Christian families, have they been baptized, taught to read, and learnt their catechism? Surely this is a duty incumbent on masters or heads of families. Sirs, if you had a sick child, would you not send for a doctor? If your house was on fire would you not strive to put it out to save your interest? Surely then you ought to use the means appointed to save the souls which God has committed to your charge, and not forget the words of Joshua, as for me and my house we will serve the Lord. Children should be taught the fear of God: See what Solomon says, Prov. viii, 18. *The fear of the Lord is to hate evil;* chapter ix, 10. *The fear of the Lord is the beginning of wisdom;* chapter xiv, 17. *The fear of the Lord is a fountain of life.* Here we see that children should fear the Lord.

But I turn to my Brethren for whom this discourse is designed. My Brethren, if ye are desirous to be saved by the merits of Jesus Christ, ye must forsake all your sins, and come to the Lord by prayer and repentance of all your former sins, come labouring and heavy laden; for we are invited to come and rely on the blessed Jesus for eternal salvation. Matthew x, 32. *Whosoever shall confess me before men, him will I confess before my heavenly father.* Here we have our Saviour's words for our encouragement. See to it my brethren, that ye live a holy life, and that ye walk more circumspect or holy than ye have done heretofore. I now assure you that God is a spirit, and they that worship him must worship him in spirit and in truth; therefore if ye would come unto him, come as the poor publican did, and say God be merciful to me a sinners; Luke xv, 11. *And the publican standing afar off would not lift up so much as his eyes unto heaven, but smote upon his breast saying, God be merciful to me a sinner.* For if we hope to be saved by the merits of Jesus Christ, we cast off all self-dependence, as to our own righteousness; for by grace ye are saved through faith, and that not of yourselves, it is the gift of God.

Here we see that the imperfections of human nature is such, that we cannot be saved by any other way but the name of Jesus Christ, and that there must be a principle of love and fear of God implanted in our hearts, if we desire to come to the divine fountain labouring and heavy laden with our sins. But the enquirer may enquire how do you prove this doctrine, are you not imposing on your brethren, as you know many of them cannot read. To this I answer, Sir, I do not mean to impose on my brethren, but to shew them there must be a principle of fear and love to God, and now I am to prove this doctrine that we ought to fear God, Psalm ciii, 11. *For as the heavens is high above the earth, so great is his mercy towards them that fear him. Verse 13. Like as a father pitieth his children, so the Lord pitieth them that fear him.* Psalm xxxiv, 9 *O fear the Lord ye his saints, for there is no want to them that fear him. Verse 11. Come ye children hearken unto me. I will teach you the fear of the Lord.* This may suffice to prove the doctrine that we ought to fear the Lord, here my brethren we see how much our salvation depends on our being transformed anew in Christ Jesus, for we are sinners by nature and are adding thereunto every day of our life, for man is prone to evil as the sparks to fly upward, this thought should put us on our guard against all manner of evil, especially of bad company. This leads me to say, we should endeavour to glorify God in all our actions whether spiritual or temporal, for the apostle hath told us whatever we do, do all to the glory of God. 1 Cor. x. 30.

Let us now labour for that food which tendeth unto eternal life, this none can give but God only: My Brethren, it is your duty to strive to make your calling and election sure by a holy life, working out your salvation with fear and trembling, for we are invited to come without money and without price.

Isaiah lv. 1 *Ho every one that thirsteth come ye to the waters; and he that hath no money, come ye buy and eat; yea come and buy wine and milk without money and without price.* This leads me to say if we suffer as sinners, under the light of the gospel as sinners, the fault is in us, for our Saviour hath told us if he had not come we should not had sin, but now they have no cloak for their sins. Let us now improve our talents by coming labouring and burthened with a sense of our sins. This certainly is a necessary duty of all mankind, to come to the divine fountain for mercy and for the influence of God's holy spirit to guide us through this wilderness to the mansions of eternal glory.

My Brethren, have we not great encouragement to come unto the Lord Jesus Christ, Matthew vii. 7. *Ask and it shall be given you, knock and it shall be opened unto you.* Therefore if ye desire to be saved by the merits of Christ, ye must come as the prodigal son did, Luke xv. 21. *And the son said unto him father I have sinned against Heaven and in thy sight and am no more worthy to be called thy son.* This is the language of the true penetent, for he is made sensible that there is no other name given by which he can be saved, but by the name of Jesus. Therefore we should put our trust in him and strive to make our calling and election sure, by prayer and meditation.

Psalm lv, 1. *Give ear to my prayer O God, and hide not thyself from my supplication.*

But, my Brethren, are we not too apt to put off the thoughts of death till we are sick, or some misfortune happens to us, forgetting that bountiful hand who gives us every good gift: Doth not the tokens of mortality call aloud to us all to prepare for death our great and last change, not flattering ourselves with the hopes of a long life, for we know not what a day may bring forth, therefore my Brethren let it be your greatest care to prepare for death, that great and irresistable king of terrors. Are we many of us advanced in years and we know not how soon God may be pleased to call us out of this life to an endless eternity, for this is the lot of all men, once to die, and after that the judgment. Let us now come to the Lord Jesus Christ, with a sense of our own impotency to do any good thing of ourselves, and with a thankful remembrance of the death of Christ who died to save lost man, and hath invited us to come to him labouring and heavy laden. My ancient Brethren, let us examine ourselves now whither we have had a saving change wrought in our hearts, and have repented of our sins, have we made it our greatest care to honor God's holy word and to keep his holy Sabbath's, and to obey his commandments.

Exodus xx. 6. *And shewing mercy to thousands of them that love me and keep my commandments,* have we been brought to how to the divine sovereignty of the Most High God and to fly to the arms of the crucified Jesus, at whose crucifiction the mountains trembled, and the rocks rent, and the graves were opened and many bodies of saints that slept arose. Come my dear fellow servants and brothers, Africans by nation, we are all invited to come, Acts x. 34. *Then Peter opened his mouth and said, of a truth I perceive that God is no respecter of persons,* verse 35, *But in every nation he that feareth him is accepted of him.* My Brethren, many of us are seeking a temporal freedom, and I wish you may obtain it; remember that all power in heaven and on earth belongs to God; if we are slaves it is by the permission of God, if we are free it must be by the power of the most high God. Stand still and see the salvation of God, cannot that same power that divided the waters from the waters for the children of Israel to pass through, make way for your freedom, and I pray that God would grant your desire, and that he may give you grace to seek that freedom which tendeth to eternal life, John viii, 32, *And ye shall know the truth and the truth shall make you free. Verse 36, If the Son shall make you free you shall be free indeed.*

This we know my brethren, that all things work together for good to them that love God. Let us manifest this love to God by a holy life.

My dear Brethren, as it hath been reported that I had petitioned to the court of Hartford against freedom, I now solemnly declare that I never have said, nor done anything, neither directly nor indirectly, to promote or to prevent freedom; but my answer hath always been I am a stranger here and I do not care to be concerned or to meddle with public affairs, and by this declaration I hope my friends will be satisfied, and all prejudice removed. Let us all strive to be united together in love, and to become new creatures, for if any man be in Christ Jesus he is a new creature, 2 Cor. v. 17. *Therefore if any man be in Christ he is a new creature* Old things are passed away behold all things are become new, now to be a new creature is to have our minds turned from darkness to light, from sin to holiness and to have a desire to serve God with our whole hearts, and to follow his precepts. Psalm xix, 10. *More to be desired than gold, yea than much fine gold, sweeter than honey and the honeycomb.* Verse 11. *Moreover by them is thy servant warned, and by keeping them there is great reward.*

Let me now, my brethren, persuade you to prepare for death by prayer and meditation, that is the way Matt. vi. *But when thou prayest enter into thy closet, and, when thou hast shut the door, pray to thy father in secret, and thy father which seeth in secret shall reward thee openly.*

My Brethren, while we continue in sin, we are enemies to Christ, ruining ourselves, and a hurt to the commonwealth.

Let us now, my brethren, come labouring and heavy laden with a sense of our sins, and let us pray that God may in his mercy be pleased to lift up the gates of our hearts, and open the doors of our souls, that the King of Glory may come in, and set these things home on our hearts. Psalm xxiv. 7. *Lift up your heads O ye gates, and be ye listed up ye everlasting doors, and the King of Glory shall come in;* then may we rely on the merits of Christ, and say, as David did, *In the Lord put I my trust,* Psalm xi. 4. And again, *whom have I in heaven but thee, and there is none on earth I desire besides thee.*

And now, my brethren, I shall endeavour to prove that we are not only ruining ourselves by sin, but many others. If the generality of men were more humble and more holy, we should not hear the little children in the street taking God's holy name in vain. Surely our conversation should be yea, yea, and nay, nay, or to that purpose. Matt. v. 7. *But let your communication be yea, yea, nay, nay, for whatsoever is more than these cometh of evil.* Therefore my Brethren, we should endeavour to walk humble and holy, to avoid the appearance of evil; to live a life void of offence towards God and towards man. Hear what David saith, Psalm I, 1. *Blessed is the man that walketh not in the counsel of ungodly nor standeth in the way of sinners.* Here we see how much it becomes us to live as Christians, not in rioting and drunkenness, uncleanness, Sabbath breaking, swearing, taking God's holy name in vain; but our delight should be in the law of the Lord.

The righteous man is compared to a tree that brength forth fruit in season. Psalm I, 3. *And he shall be like a tree planted by the rivers of water, that bringeth forth fruit in his season: His leaf also shall not wither, and whatsoever he doeth shall prosper.* Let us not forget the words of holy David, *man is but dust like the flower of the field.* Psalm ciii, 15.

Let us remember the uncertainty of human life, and that we are many of us within a step of the grave, hanging only by the single thread of life, and we know not how soon God may send the cold hand of death and cut the thread of life: Then will our souls either ascend up to the eternal mansions of glory or descend down to eternal misery, our bodies lodged in the cold and silent grave, numbered with the dead, then shall the scripture be fulfilled, Gen. iii, 19. *In the sweat of thy face shalt thou eat bread, till thou return to the ground, for out of it wast thou taken, for dust thou art and unto dust thou shalt return.*

Now I am to call to the unconverted, my brethren, if we desire to become true converts, we must be born again, we must have a spiritual regeneration. John iii, 3. *Verily, verily, I say unto you, except a man be born again he cannot see the kingdom of God.*

My brethren, are we not, many of us, ignorant of this spiritual regeneration? Have we seen our lost and undone condition without an interest in the merits of Jesus Christ; have we come weary and heavy laden without sins, and to say with holy David, Psalm vi. 10. *Lord rebuke me not in thine anger, neither chasten me in thy hot displeasure.* Hath it been our great care to prepare for death our great and last change, by prayer and meditation.

My dear brethren, though we are servants and have not so much time as we could wish for, yet we must improve the little time we have.

Mr. Burket, a great divine of our church, says, a man's hand may be on his plow and his heart in heaven, by putting up such prayers and exclamations as these, Psalm lxi. 1. *Hear my cry O God, attend to my prayer,* and again, *whom have I in heaven but thee, and there is none on earth I desire besides thee.*

We should pray that God would give us his holy spirit, that we may not be led into temptation, and that we may be delivered from evil, especially the evil of sin. Rom. vi. 22, 23. *But now, being made free from sin, and become servants of God, ye have your fruit unto holiness, and the end everlasting life. For the wages of sin is death, but the gift of God is eternal life through Jesus Christ our Lord.*

My brethren, seeing I am desired by my friends to write something more than poetry, give me leave to speak plainly to you. Except you repent and forsake your sins ye must surely die. Now we see how much it becomes us to break our alliance with sin and Satan, and to fly to a crucified Saviour, and to enlist under

Christ's banner, and that he may give us grace to become his faithful subjects, should be our constant prayers. We should guard against every sin, especially against bad language.

Therefore, my Brethren, we should always be guarding against every evil word, for we are told that the tongue is an evil member, for with the tongue we bless God, and with the tongue we curse men. 1 Peter iii. 10. For he that loves life, and would see good days, let him refrain his tongue from evil and his lips from speaking guile. But the thoughtless and unconverted sinner is going on in open rebellion, against that divine power which can in one minute cut the thread of life, and cast them away with this pronunciation, Depart from me ye workers of iniquity. Matt. xxv. 41. *Then shall be say also unto them on the left hand, depart from me ye cursed into everlasting fire prepared for the devil and his angels.*

And now, my brethren, shall we abuse the divine sovereignty of a holy God, who hath created us rational creatures, capable of serving him under the light of the Gospel, for he hath told us if he had not come unto us we had not had sin, but now we have no cloak for our sin.

Come now my dear brethren, accept of Jesus Christ on the terms of the gospel, which is by faith and repentance. Come labouring and heavy laden with your sins, and a sense of your unworthiness.

My Brethren, it is not we servants only that are unworthy, but all mankind by the fall of Adam, became guilty in the sight of God. Gen. ii. 17. Surely then we are sinners by nature, and are daily adding thereto by evil practices, and it is only by the merits of Jesus Christ we can be saved, we are told that he is a Jew that is a Jew in his heart, so he is a Christian that is a Christian in his heart, and it is not every one that says Lord, Lord, shall enter into the kingdom of God, but he that doth the will of God. Let our superiors act as they shall think it best, we must resolve to walk in the steps our Saviour hath set before us, which was a holy life, a humble submission to the will of God. Luke xxii. 41, 42. *And he was withdrawn from them about a stones cast, and he kneeled down and prayed saying, father if thou be willing remove this cup from me, nevertheless not my will but thine be done.*

Here we have the example of our Saviour who came down from heaven to save mankind, lost and undone without an interest in the merits of Jesus Christ, the blessed Jesus then gave his life a ransom for all that come unto him by faith and repentance; and shall not he that spared not his own son, but delivered him up for us all, with him freely give all things.

Come let us seek first, Christ, the kingdom of God; and his righteousness, all other things shall be added unto you. Matt. vi. 33. Here we have great encouragement to come to the divine fountain.

Bishop Beverage says, in his third resolution, the eyes of the Lord are intent upon us, he seeth our actions; if our sins are not washed out with our tears, and croft with the blood of Christ, we cannot be saved. Come my brethren, O taste and see that the Lord is good, and blessed is the man that trusted in him. Psalm xxxiv. 8. Let us not stand as Felix did, and say, almost thou persuadest me to be a Christian, but, let us strive to be altogether so. If ye desire to become converts you must have a saving change wrought in your hearts that shall bring forth good works meet for repentance: Acts iii. 19. Repent ye therefore, be converted: We are not to trust in our own strength but to trust in the Lord; Proverbs iii, 4. "Trust in the Lord with all thine heart and lean not unto thine own understanding."

My brethren, are we not incircled with many temptations, the flesh, the world and the devil; these must be resisted at all times. We must see to it that we do not grieve the holy spirit of God. Come let us my dear brethren, draw near to the Lord by faith and repentance, for faith without works is dead. James ii. 20. and Rom. x, 10. For with the heart man believed, and with the mouth confession is made unto salvation. Here we see there is something to be done by us as Christians; therefore we should walk worthy of our profession, not forgetting that there is a divine power which takes a just survey of all our actions, and will reward every one according to their works. Psalm lxii, 2. "Also unto the Lord belongeth mercy, for thou rememberest every man according to his works." Therefore, it is our indispensable duty to improve all opportunities to serve God, who gave us his only son to save all that come unto him by faith and repentance.

Let me, my brethren, persuade you to a serious consideration of your danger while you continue in an unconverted state. Did you feel the operations of God's holy spirit, you then would leave all for an interest in the merits of Christ; "For the kingdom of heaven is like a treasure hid in a field; for which a man will fell all that he hath to purchase, Matt. x. 44. So will every true penitent part with all for the sake of Christ I shall not attempt to drive you to Christ by the terrors of the law, but I shall endeavour to allure you by the invitation of the gospel, to come labouring and heavy laden.

Matt. xi. 27. Man at his best estate is like a shadow of the field. We should always be preparing for death, not having our hearts set on the things of this life: For what profit will it be to us, to pain the whole world and loose his own soul. Matt. xvi. 26. We should be always preparing for the will of God, working out our salvation with fear and trembling. O may we abound in the works of the Lord. Let us not stand as fruitless trees or cumberers of the ground, for by your works you shall be justified, and by your works you shall be condemned; for every man shall be rewarded according to his works, Matt. xvi. 27. Let us then be pressing forward to the mark, for the prize of the high calling of God in Christ Jesus. Let our hearts be fixed where true joys are to be found. Let us lay up treasures in Heaven where neither moth nor rust doth corrupt, not thieves break through nor steal. Matt. vi. 20.

Now I am come to contemplate the death of Christ, it remains I make a short contemplation. The death of Christ who died! Died to save lost man, 1 Cor. xv. 21. "For since by man came death, by man came also the resurrection from the dead: For as in Adam all died even so in Christ, shall all be made alive.

Let us turn to the scriptures, and there we shall see how our Saviour was denied by one and betrayed by another. Matt. xxvi, 14. Judas went unto the Chief Priest, and said, what will you give me, and they agreed for thirty pieces of silver, then they sought opportunity to betray him. Verse 28. For this is my blood of the New Testament, which is shed for many for the remission of sins. Ver. 33. Peter answered and said unto him, though all men should be offended because of thee, yet will I never be offended. Ver. 34. Jesus said unto him, verily I say unto thee, this night before the cock crow, thou shalt deny me thirce. Ver. 38, Then faith he unto them, my soul is exceeding sorrowful, even unto death: tarry ye here and watch with me Ver. 39. And he went a little further and fell on his face and prayed, saying, O Father, if it be possible, let this cup pass from me: Nevertheless not as I will, but as thou wilt.

My Brethren, here we see the love of God plainly set before us; that while we were yet sinners, he sent his son to die for all those that come unto him, labouring and heavy laden with a sense of their sins; let us come with a thankful remembrance of his death, whose blood was shed for us guilty worms of the dust. Mat. xxvi. 69. But Jesus held his peace, and the High Priest answered and said unto him, I adjure thee by the Living God, that thou tell us, whether thou be the Christ the son of God. And ver. 64. Jesus faith unto him, thou hast said: nevertheless I say unto you, hereafter shall ye see the Son of Man sitting on the right hand of power, and coming in the clouds of heaven. Ver. 64. Then the High Priest rent his clothes, saying, he hath spoken blasphemy; what further need have we of witness? Behold, now ye have heard his blasphemy. Here the High Priest charged the blessed Jesus with blasphemy: But we must believe that he is able to save all that come unto him, by faith and repentance. Matt. xxviii. 18. And Jesus came and spoke unto them, saying, all power is given unto me in heaven and on earth. As this should excite us to love and fear God, and to strive to keep his holy commandments, which is the only rule of life: But how apt are we to forget that God spoke these words, saying, I am the Lord thy God, which brought thee out of the land of Egypt and out of the house of bondage, Exod. xx. 1. Thus we see how the children of Israel were delivered from the Egyptian service.

But my Brethren, we are invited to the blessed Jesus, who was betrayed by one and denied by another. Matt. xx. 24. The Son of Man goeth as it is written of him; but woe unto that man by whom the Son of Man is betrayed; it had been good for that man if he had never been born. Ver. 24. Then Judas which betrayed him answered and said, Master is it I? He said unto him, thou hast said.

Thus we see, my Brethren, that there is a woe pronounced against every one that sins by omission or commission, are we not going on in our sins, and disobeying the word of God: "If ye love me, ye will keep my commandments." Are we not denying the Lord Jesus, as Peter did. Matt. xxvi. 14. Then began he to curse and swear, saying, I know not the man; and immediately the cock crew. And ver. 74. And Peter remembered the words of Jesus, which he said unto him, before the cock crow thou shalt deny me thrice: And he went out and wept bitterly. Surely then we ought to come to the Divine Sovereign, the blessed

Jesus who was crucified for us sinners. Oh! we ought to come on the bended knees of our souls, and say, Lord, we believe, help thou our unbelief. Come my Brethern, let us cry to the life-giving Jesus, and say, Son of God, have mercy on us! Lamb of God, that taketh away the sins of the world, have mercy on us! Let us cast off all self-dependence and rely on a crucified Saviour. Luke xxiii. 20. Pilate therefore, willing to release Jesus, spoke again to them. Ver. 21. But they cried, saying, crucify him, crucify him. Here we may see the love of God, in giving his Son to save all that come unto him by faith and repentance. Let us trace the sufferings of our Saviour a little further: Matt. xxvi. 42. He went away again the second time, and prayed, saying, O my Father, if this cup may not pass away from me, except I drink it, thy will be done. Here we trace our Saviour's example set before us; so that we should not murmur at the hand of Divine Providence; for God hath a right to deal with his creatures as he pleased.

Come let us contemplate on the death of the blessed Jesus; and on the fearful judgment of the Lord passing on the guilty sinner. Luke xxiii. 30. Then shall they begin to say to the mountains, fall on us, and to the hills, cover us. Ver. 32, 33. And there were also two malefactors led with him to be put to death; and when they were come to the place, which is called Calvary, there they crucified him and the malefactors, one on the right hand, and the other on the left; and thus was the scripture fulfilled: For he was numbered with transgressors. Matt. xxvii. 29. And when they had plated a crown of thorns, they put it upon his head, and a reed in his right hand. Ver. 41, 42. Likewise the Chief Priests mocking him, with the Scribes and Elders, said, he saved others, himself he cannot save: If he be the king of Israel, let him come down from the cross, and we will believe him. Ver. 44. Now from the sixth hour there was darkness over all the land unto the ninth hour. Ver. 46. And about the ninth hour Jesus cried with a loud voice, saying, Eli, Eli, Lama Sabachthani! That is to say, my God, my God, why hast thou forsaken me?

My brethern, should not a sense of these things on our mind implant in us a spirit of love to God, which hath provided a Saviour, who is able to save to the uttermost all that come unto him by faith and repentance 2. Cor. vii. 10. For Godly sorrow worketh repentance to salvation, not to be repented of, but the sorrow of the world worketh death. My brethren, see what sin hath done; it hath made all flesh guilty in the sight of God.

May we not adopt the language of David. Psal. lxxx 8. O remember not against us former iniquities. Let thy tender mercies speedily prevent us. Psal. lxxx 19. Turn us again, O Lord, God of Hosts, cause thy face to shine, and we shall be saved.

Let us contemplate a little further on the death of Christ. Matt. xxvii. 40. Jesus, when he had cried with a loud voice, yielded up the ghost. Ver. 4, And behold the vail of the temple was sent in twain, from the top to the bottom; and the earth did quake, and the rocks rent. Here we see that the death of Christ caused all nature to tremble, and the power of heaven shaken: Here we may see not only the evil of sin, but also the unmeritted mercy of God, in giving his only Son. Should not our hearts be filled with sear and love to God; and we must believe that Jesus is the Son of God. Matt. xxvii. 54. Now when the Centurion and they that were with him, watching Jesus saw the earthquake, and those things that were done, they feared greatly, saying, truly this was the Son of God. Now this was done for the remission of our sins, for without shedding of blood there is no remission of sin. This we have confirmed in the holy sacrament. Matt. xxvi. 27. For this is my blood of the New Testament, which was shed for many: But the unbelieving Jews still persisted in their unbelief, and would have prevented the resurrection of our Saviour, if it had been in their power. Matt. xxvii. 62. The Chief Priests and Pharisees come together unto Pilate. Ver. 63, Saying, Sir, we remember that that deceiver said, while he was yet alive, after three days I will rise again. Ver. 66. So they went and made the sepulchre sure, sealing the stone and setting a watch. Here we see the spirit of unbelief in Nathaniel. John I. 45 and 46. Philip findeth Nathaniel, and faith unto him, we have found him, of whom Moses in the law and the prophets did write, Jesus of Nazareth, the son of Joseph: And Nathaniel said unto him, can there any good thing come out of Nazareth? Philip faith unto him, come and see. Thus we are to come and see the mercy of God, in sending his Son to save lost men. Let us contemplate on the manner of Christ's resurrection. Matt. xxv. 2. Behold there was a great earthquake; for the angel of the Lord descended from heaven, and came and rolled the stone from the door, and sat upon it. Here we see that our Saviour was attended by an angel; one of those holy spirits we read of in the Revelations, vi. 8. They rest not day and night, saying, holy, holy, holy Lord God Almighty, which was and is, and is to come. Ver. 4, 12. Saying, with a loud voice, worthy is the Lamb, that was slain, to receive power and riches, and wisdom, and strength, and honor, and glory, and blessing. And our Saviour himself tells us he hath received his power. Matt. xxviii 19. And Jesus came and spoke unto them, saying, all power is given unto me in heaven and in earth. Then he gives his disciples their charge. Ver. 19. Go ye, therefore, and teach all nations, baptizing them in the name of the Father, of the Son, and of the Holy Ghost. But I must conclude in a few words, and say,

My dear Brethren, should we not admire the free grace of God, that he is inviting of us to come and accept of Jesus Christ, on the terms of the gospel; and he is calling us to repent of all our sins: This we cannot do of ourselves, but we must be saved in the use of means not to neglect those two great articles of the Christian religion, baptism and the sacrament; and we ought all of us to seek by prayers: But the scripture hath told us, that we must not depend on the use of means alone. 1st Cor. iii. 6. The apostle says, I have planted Apolos watered, but God gave the increase. Here we see if we are saved, it must be by the power of God's holy spirit. But my dear Brethren the time is hastening when we must appear.

A Note About the Author

Jupiter Hammon (1711–1806) was an African American poet and preacher. Born into slavery at Lloyd Manor on Long Island, New York, Hammon was educated by the Anglican Church and developed a talent for reading and writing at a young age. In 1761, his poem "An Evening Thought: Salvation by Christ, with Penitential Cries" was published as a broadside, making Hammon the first Black published author in American history. During the Revolutionary War, he composed "An Address to Miss Phillis Wheatley," which appeared in print eighteen years after his debut. In 1786, at the inaugural assembly of the African Society in New York City, Hammon delivered a speech titled "Address to the Negroes in the State of New York." At 76 years old, still enslaved by the Lloyd family, he affirmed his faith in heavenly salvation and stated his hope for the freedom of future generations. He lived an astounding life, inspiring many and defying his captivity in subtle acts of resistance. Although his work is limited—four poems and four prose pieces—Hammon displayed a mastery of Christian theology and poetic form while pursuing a message of racial uplift and moral righteousness. Buried in an unmarked grave, enslaved for the entirety of his life on earth, Jupiter Hammon remains an insurmountable force in American history and a pioneer of African American literature.

A Note from the Publisher

Spanning many genres, from non-fiction essays to literature classics to children's books and lyric poetry, Mint Edition books showcase the master works of our time in a modern new package. The text is freshly typeset, is clean and easy to read, and features a new note about the author in each volume. Many books also include exclusive new introductory material. Every book boasts a striking new cover, which makes it as appropriate for collecting as it is for gift giving. Mint Edition books are only printed when a reader orders them, so natural resources are not wasted. We're proud that our books are never manufactured in excess and exist only in the exact quantity they need to be read and enjoyed.

bookfinity™

Discover more of your favorite classics with Bookfinity™.

- Track your reading with custom book lists.
- Get great book recommendations for your personalized Reader Type.
- Add reviews for your favorite books.
- AND MUCH MORE!

Visit **bookfinity.com** and take the fun Reader Type quiz to get started.

Enjoy our classic and modern companion pairings!

Classic & Modern

www.ingramcontent.com/pod-product-compliance
Lightning Source LLC
Chambersburg PA
CBHW020605030426
42337CB00013B/1219